WHEN LIFE BIGHTS

SIMRAN KAUR NOKWAL

BlueRose Publishers

First Published in November 2020

ISBN: 978-93-5427-052-9

BLUEROSE PUBLISHERS

www.bluerosepublishers.com

info@bluerosepublishers.com

+91 8882 898 898

Cover Design:

Joshua Freitas

Typographic Design:

Namrata Saini

Distributed by: BlueRose, Amazon, Flipkart, Shopclues

DEDICATION

When the whole world is muffled into COVID-19 pandemic, I'm no exception. I too lost many near and dear ones that actually prompted my rationale towards the pith of being. This book is a humble attempt to jot down my understanding and my perspective of life, heretofore. So yes ! I dedicate this book to all of them.

But even to those who are with me in this rugged times and helping me moulding my amateur thoughts into something better.

CONTENTS

TIME

Oh time oh time! When will you come,
Can't state my lost mind in one sum

Oh time oh time! When will you come,
Tired withstanding the life that makes me so dumb

Oh time oh time! When will you come,
Gazing in the air for ace happy chunk

Oh time oh time! When will you come,
Shower tad wisdom through some pump

Oh time oh time when will you come,
Save me from fiend & take that lump

Oh time oh time! When will you come,
Yes that's right, from my inner demon

Oh time oh time! When will you come,
Can't stay long in this wild unbridled scrum

Oh time oh time! When will you come,
Heart is sinking and sinking out of plum

Oh time oh time! When will you come,
Can't state my lost mind in one sum.

ALONE IS WHAT

Alone is what, that makes you boring?
Careful lad! choose word that's scoring,

Alone is what, that gives you chills?
Per diem an opportunity that may thrill,

Alone is what, no partner in crime?
Become the hero and aim to prime,

Alone is what, no ally to lionise?
Truth of life often come in disguise,

Alone is what, no communion of pain?
Fortitude to zig when others' zag is what one gain,

Alone is what, do you know it's worth?
Discovering self that blossom forth,

Alone is what, will you be spared?
Life seldom throws opportunity, one better be prepared,

Alone is what, you seriously alone?
Time for cogitation that needs to hone,

Alone is what? It's a lesson learnt hard
Beware friends! Now I know my cards.

LIPSTICK

When my diem is slow and I'm bearing low,
Having you on, makes my circadian glow

Cherry lush, Pirate, Ruby for me,
And so I'm semper alive be

I marvel why populist despite you,
Utterly crave yet flagrantly despise you,
Bliss that I get, so Intrinsic you

With you I convey even my unspeakables,
No matter how many names I get in my labels,
You are my fillip that keeps me dementedly stable

Not just my lips, waiting my eyes and cheeks,
Savvy I turn, put quis up the creek

The pain I get & feel so sick,
Ever don't get knotted, you my lipstick.

"C" FOR CORPORATE

A for apple, B for ball and C for corporate,
Ignorant of that world, I was till date

How to behave and how to cooperate,
Oh god! Tell me am I that late?

Nicely dressed and full of etiquettes,
Nonpareil their skills, often get me scare,
Diplomatic ad-nauseam, now that's what I hate

Who is who and in leisure what they do,
Sneak into everything, that I simply boo

A line is drawn and a limit not to cross,
Who will teach them, coz its totally gross

Talks are artificial and world so fake,
Lies per diem, are what they bake

Its worrisome if this is our today and future,
TOUT DE SUITE to make alteration in our nature

I swear word to clean my surround,
Spick and span, it is to which I'm bound

Few miles walking away from home,
Lo and behold ! Its me to be hone

A jerky dreadful feeling arrive in spate,
It's time to call spade a spade

A place to provide an opportunity to breathe,
Where thoughts are welcome and speech is freed
habitare that accommodative, irrespective of creed

Oh my ! Assist me where I'm wrong,
Position my attitude and take me along

Render me strength and refine my thoughts,
I pursue you for the wisdom I sought

I adhere to the point that work is worship,
Make me capable to take that ship

If not much, leastwise stay with me,
Guide me with sapience is what I plea

World of corporate is full of opportunity,
Shrewd enough to reconnaissance in continuity

Propel to incorporate which is highly intricate,
Cosmo is the word which is corporate.

MOTHERS

A soul that sees from the eyes of heart,
Near or far, she teneo her divine art

A sight that makes you forget your pain,
A touch that let your negan's drain

A feel is felt, filled with her pureness,
Scared that alliance, she grapple to harness

Aukat meri kaha ki mai kuj likh paun,
Rabb se Pehle sau baar Jiska naam dhiyaun

Bonus aut malus, her love is limitless,
Forfeiting her comfort, her existence is seamless

True it is, pauci souls are not described,
Poor my words that fail to ascribe.

I'M NEW

Should you cared to ask just once,
I would have let my heart out on that stance

Waiting for your asseveration like forever,
I was holding on to you, thinking shall together get it over

If not now, then when, comes to my mind in rewind,
Occurrence of ego and divest loaded in combine

Thoroughly living the moment, though I was
loosing somewhere,
When you did bounce on me, like you don't care

Basked every moment spend with you in clear,
No matter if it lead me to the itinerary of smear

My fall happened in a blink of an eye,
As my choices took a body, on whom I may semper rely

Never met anyone close to your mentation,
Gosh ! what was that, I still miss those orations

The night in the concert when we laughed our lungs out,
Hankering to take you inside me then and there, even for
bout

Soon my immature bubble burst as I talk
through one's hat,
Impinge on my true grade, as it comes in stat

Oh mine! It was not and never your fault,
Love often happens, and happens in default

Now that I don't have much of you to hold on,
I ask God for your prosperitas, from dark to dawn

Not a dedication, but I hereby vent, to move in peace,
Anything can happen in life, one just have to see

AB IRATO

They say what a mind can conceive, it can achieve,
Certainly! today however my thoughts are cleave

I hover worriedly, what are we upto?
coz, we could definitely have otherwise, in lieu

From the life by choices to the life by chances, indeed we have come a long way,
Humans! the living disaster is ready to hold sway
With our bare hands, inditing tales of macabre

Yes ! there is a distinction between animals and me,
They don't have choices and I'm not worthy

Threat to my own kind, I am threat to nature,
Tasting my own medicine, I am no a creator

Hurricanes, earthquakes, wildfire and cyclones,
Ensuant of our actions, we better rest alone

Becoming the master, he who holds nothing,
Incognisant of his irreparable deeds, will be thrown far from the sling

Underestimating the power of "haves", inter-alia we
surpasses the word rapacious,
When will it be stopped ! long way of being satiable

What train of thoughts are we carrying?
Are we educated and hollow in knowledge or functionally
illiterate brimmed in degrees?

Jealousy, cupidity, contention won't lead us
anywhere,
World of collaboration not competition, is thought to spare

Lacking deliberation and ministration, we stand on the
verge of destruction,
Oh humans ! time immemorial of your humanisation

ill at ease, he who cannot see the status quo,
Bear in mind the acts of omission and commission, else rue

No time to sling mud inter-se,
If there is a will, there is a way

If cannot create, at least don't spifflicate,
You owe to nature, not contra-wise is a seed to militate

MUSIC

A string of you, makes me stand on cloud nine,
Exultant I become even more then fine

The synchrony of beats pump in my heart,
Nature has divine ways to bestow its art

The twitter, whistle, cluck and caw,
Insouciantly melodious, so intrinsic raw

Pondering I semper, the essence of this euphony,
Beyond the boundaries, approximation many

A bandage to wound, a breath to submerged,
Salvator to multi, standing on the verge

Lost in this tumult, I seek assistance,
Cling with you, I shall forever in patience

Adding melody to my speech and rhythm to my chore,
Like a dulcet tones of tides bumping to a shore

I may call you water without which there is no life,
Nescient of this therapy, I would have dived

With every single chord strikes deep into my heart,
Lustre my mundanes with its spine-tingling
chanted arc

Like a seamless flow of blood in my veins,
You get subsumed spiritually, with all its reins

Lets traverse, where there is harmony,
You the treasure to possess, worthy right
on the money

You arc in my felicity, you are my prayers,
United with you, my music of spheres.

BETTER DARE TO

Its apha to winnow out from being in that billet,
Then staying at disposition and let them cut
you into filets

Stand and walk away to anything but this,
Won't get another chance if not now you dismiss

Yes it's hazy, how it will and how far it will?
Leurn to mount a hillock which metier to mickle

Coz, what's the fun in the path otherwise?
Surely, if dealing in derisory and not getting a tad wise

Ask the one who dint even taste a bargain price,
As brusquely they refuse to uprise

Yes perhaps! It's the time, don't impasse
keep rowing,
As they say when going gets tough, the tough
gets going

Don't let your courage blip and heart to sink,
Dare to be unploughed and refuse that kink

As who are they to turn your pink into pale,
Ever don't let zephyr abandon your dale

But oh chap! What's the point of reaching up there
all so bruised?
With thoughts so traduced and mind contuse.

And as I picked this dare, it's a requital in return
Its mere an art in which way you turn,
Do it at ease or dampen in concern

But surely stand and walk away to anything
but this,
As life is myriad of daring compositions it
may consist.

COSMETICS

Amid of such crises, I sense how you postulate,
Agazing quietly, wanting to be mate

But ! you my accessories, hope you understand,
Bear with me, I shall never leave you strand

Recalling the times when I used to wear you,
Boost my confidence and never seek your due
You become my strength in the times of blue

Well-versed that populist ascribe you disdainfully,
But I'm cognisant of your worth, can't let your reputation sully

Ask earnestly my eyes, cheeks and ears,
Without you, my diem walks in first gear

Cornered in my shelf, I sense your pain,
My spirit is low, trust me! Nor do I gain

Oh my cosmetics ! Don't get run out or dry,
Let's hold together this vigor, C'mon! lets try

Time soon come, will become again mutualist,
You become prime with my amor hand over fist

Remember ! without you my life is fractional,
You are my epitome of silent interactional.

A JOURNEY OF YOU AND ME

Sitting at a corner of my room, I mull what has happened,
Devising deeply apprehensively an attitude that needs to append

They told, my vibes are not okay,
People gets dithery, closing my self-seeker ray

Remembering of days when they chose me,
Ignorant of that sensum, I was jumping gladly like a bee

Dreaming that I will bloom,
Will gain a lot, like a wisdom weaving on a loom

Gazing at the world that has opened its wide arms to me,
Like a go-getter, I subsume the chances that were once may be

Brimming with valour, confidence and fidelis, I landed in a place,
Slowly and steadily I was footing towards building my pace

Appreciated when good, rebuked when failed, was amassing
that experience,
With the hope inside me that yes! I possess tad expedience

Consciously I was adorning my persona,
Crude I was, tardily elevating this fauna

Lo and behold ! It is a world not fair,
No option given, one picks that dare

No theorem, no formula applies to this,
Perpetually judged, either treated well or diss

To this point I believe, I chose my choice,
Its my selection, I pother or rejoice

Who are they and what they mean,
I refuse to care and refuse to lean

Blessed with this life, sky's the limit,
Only I possess the power to make my decision licit

Versed with the fact that it's easy said than done,
But I'm my queen hence, I refuse to give up

Focusing on self-growth, that pays sooner or later,
The physical and mental wellness is just I need to cater

Yes ! World is bitch and so is bountied,
Art of enduring hard knocks with courage is
all one need

If it's not easy for me, it's not for any,
Accounting foe and friends carefully, else be zany
Coz, it's a journey, a journey of you and me!

This phase of life has just begun,
Meddling with hypocrisy, a line well drawn
Terminus ad quem is known, cannot let it dun

Wish to be "paras", aspire to reach that focal,
Mightily turn a stone into gold, that I semper revel

IT IS WHAT IT IS!

i

They say, I frown, that its real,
The whole thought seem irrational and surreal

They exert, without which a life is incomplete,
Straightway coming from heart, not an object to compete

Pursuant to this, I ponder about its existence,
Little that I know, is it sincere of just pretence?

Curious to know more, this thought drilled in me,
Manifested from my demeanour, it hanged to
me limply

Crazy I was becoming to incur that feel
Losing myself, becoming careen,
Realising this vacuous, ok ! I am done being meek

Forget about that sense-datum, I doubt whether
it exists,
But as they say, it is what it is

I travel, eat and sleep, what else do I need,
Yet there is a void, deep inside me, that requires utmost
heed

ii

Oblivion I was, until the day we met
Is it what it is? or I simply let,
An unusual divine sentience arrived, that I do bet

A word of appreciation, a smile or perhaps your sight,
Splendour my day with mirth, like a sprite

Stimulated! I move forth and join this excursion,
Yes indeed! Au fait with an esteemed conversion

A splash of inner warts and all dampened me,
Good or evil, I am resting on the spot with the lee

I nod ! This feel exists, without which a life is incomplete,
Fine! I understand, it is what it is

However, a version of mine is different from yours
The shell is as delicate as its core,
The game more is of sustain than of scores

He who says, we are heaven-sent that makes us loveable,
In spades! It's vice-versa, to the highest degree must be
perceivable

Neither a one diem gesture, it takes you along,
Nor a terminus, it's a journey that keeps you warm

I consentio, that life is incomplete without it,
Kith and kin and friends being co-riders doing their bit

Cannot be calibrated and not to be quantified,
High or low, they hold fast with you in a tide

They are treasure chest, cannot afford to pretermit,
Without which life is truly incomplete,
Coz, it is what it is.

LENTA VITAE

They make you belittle all the time,
Thinking, it will win them their diem

Transcendency and putting under the thumb, is all they serve,
Too puerile to understand, is what gets me on my nerve

I smirk on this conundrum,
Am I a novice or are they being too accomplished?

Primo, they pull you down stating how feckless you are,
Suck your confidence and laugh at your diffidence up to par

Abducting the opportunities and demeaning on your oeuvre,
Tough becomes toughest, when it comes without knocking the door

Backed by none, this battleground becomes empty when
needed the most,
Rather relishing the flick, far from the coast

I am fetching my piecemeal as to what it takes,
It's not what rather "who" said is what I mark to make

There is no such talk or site as right or wrong,
Only he knows its summus contingent upon

No one stands in this iter, but you!
Behold what a mind can conceive, one can achieve it too

Remember! your journey is different from others,
Don't let your aim adrift and commitment withers

If not much, leastwise be truthful to inner self,
Coz, as they say! before one know the world, one should know thyself

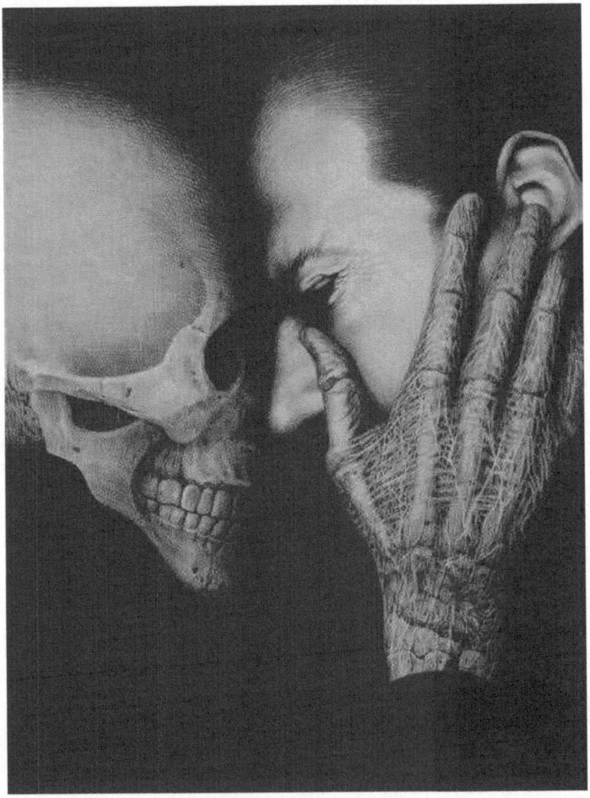

LOOSING THE ONE

When the reality hits hard that you resist to acknowledge
by hitting even harder,
When you dare to question the sun,
When you are burning ab intra but fails to stop the rain of
your eyes,
When you want to let everyone knows your pain with your
sealed lips,
When you are armata potentia, yet unable and undirected,
When the unquiet of your heart makes you quiet evermore,
When the flashback of the thoughts makes reality
obliterate,
When you dare to do that can't be done

You have lost the one !!!

(In memory of my late Brother-in-law, who we lost dated June 05, 2020 and my late Aunt, dated Sep 09, 2020)

MONEY

Money oh money! So thaumaturgical,
Yield the power that makes indignus reputable

Capacity to change the outlook of the world,
Come hell or high water, makes thou favoured

The courage to dream rooted from shekels in pocket,
Such like an unwary kiddo putting hands in socket

Spell the cast that surge thy stature among compeers,
He who doesn't even belong becomes inductee in the spheres

What an influence and what an attitude,
Changing the perspective, no matter how bruised

Behold my friends! Money has imperium to buy
even truth,
Ask the one, who tasted the world firstly in his youth

Money oh money! Do you know what I like about you?
The authority, audacity and fiducia you endue,
So ephemeral, yet assist to pursue

Ability to heal broken relations,
Ask the one, who brings home the
bacon with elation

Inducing incessant courage, Drives one even in blues,
Opening the gates of opportune, might ensues

Refuse to comrade for long with fools,
What a kick-ass true-to-life tool, that we
ought to school

Goes without saying thou Impart tough life-lessons,
Who is who's ? Go forth who deserves to be
taken in progression

Adage well said - if money buys love, it is not love, if
money buys respect, it is not respect,
He who knows thy art, may now choose his prospect

Thy possession explores wide range of possible spectrum of
life,
Power to change the future course of actions, only he who
knows what it's like!!!

RIM RIM RAIN

Rim Rim Rain O' Rim Rim Rain,
The droplets typify of fresh start, we must that attain

Rim Rim Rain O' Rim Rim Rain
That mizzle touching my cutis, let my daylong phlegm drain,
Bringing gladden ab abundantiam, like a first sip of champagne

Rim Rim Rain O' Rim Rim Rain
Skimpy my words, how can I explain,
Ask farmerette and the livestock she sustain
Like a zephyr walking through her lane,
That one morsel of dough is all she gain

Rim Rim Rain O' Rim Rim Rain
Ask that bud that's ready to blossom,
Grass gets greener and ready to colossal
Sapling gear to effloresce, yearning like an apostle

Rim Rim Rain O' Rim Rim Rain,
Greeting wide open trunks that are unrestrained

Rim Rim Rain O' Rim Rim Rain
Your lightening and thunder epitomises a
heavenly acquaintance,
Echoing the gospel while clutching in the guidance

Rim Rim Rain O' Rim Rim Rain
From microbes to Craniates, all set out to reign,
Like a majesty, looking after its glen

Rim Rim Rain O' Rim Rim Rain,
Don't Let Your Power Go In Vain

Strike where it is needed that hold omnis sane
Be the blessing in the clip of profane,
Come along with spe, time and again
Rim Rim Rain O' Rim Rim Rain

STATUS QUO

Gawping around with my intuitive feeling, today so wretched,
Where existence become impugnable and recoiling survival of the fittest,
Beyond one's stature and devoid of that crutch

Rebuffing the essence of this life time, we are around the bend,
Everything at stake, is this how we conspire to end?

A conundrum reverberating in my mind,
Why lothing to taste your own medicine that once laid for your own kind?
Mightily turning your actions, which factually unjustified!

Oh humans! Do you realise when humanity glided by?
When the quest is unwarranted, the pursuit gets diluted
When the aim is flawed, the path would never be blue-fruited,
With the volition to conquer, that can never be owned

Today the fulcrum of our deeds reached beyond the pale,
Mired in this ailment, look around! now there is no escape.

A CASE LIKE SUITCASE

If a true friend is to be defined,
you my pal, occurs to my mind

No questions, no demands and sine complaints,
Mutely you play along, In my mundane

In my thick and thin, only you appears to be a solution,
Stretch forth the arms, you let to your submission

Reckoning on each other, you subsume my clobber,
Wrap my favourites, you save me from askew

My suitcase! I wish I could steer my life like your steering wheels,
Breaking all the conventions like a dirty heel
Qui vive the world with my ageing peal

It's been a while, we consort with each other,
Sulky I am becoming, to make you bother

Holding your hand grip, you amplify my charms to scout,
Whichever colour I choose you in, you make my excursion smooth out

You are one that accessory that I love to flaunt,
Never get slaked, semper prepare to mount

Mind please! We have millions miles to go,
Till then my friend, let's move with the flow.

NOBODY MOVE
Fb.com/MinionQuotes
DespicableMeMinions.org
i JUST LOST MY
MiND.

MY ENERVATE MIND

Why you behave in an uncanny way,
when needed the most you bluntly sway,

You are aware, how dependent I am on you,
Pulling up stakes on me, seriously you too!!!

Can't you stand still when I decide to work on a thing?
Poor my concentration, can't even calibrate a fling

Distracting from the core, I end up talking
to myself,
Trying vexed reaching the focal with ELF

If I do this, I think of that
When I think of this, I forget to do that,
Noetically I intromit, you are such a f**king brat!

They say you have ability to control anatomical structure,
Perturbed of you taking advantage, even at the point of juncture

You make me numb and insult my comprehension,
Give tongue to them, to ruminate my reflection

All I ask is ataraxis to repose on,
Take your time and don't whizz along

I beg of you! Stay with me dead on the target,
With you spring to mind, I shall culminate once that I set

YES! ANGEL EXISTS

Yes it's real honest-to-goodness that angel exists,
Realises most when imbruing in problems hand over fists

That intangible deific force pulls you out,
When even kerfuffle itself decide to scout
And your courage is up the spout

So evanescence, they don't exist to stay,
Merely keeps you from your problem miles away

A sight unseen and a light untraversed is all they show,
Before vapoursing on the hot pan like a pellet of snow

From where they come and where they go,
What point to object as long as you glow

Oh! That tincture is unfading and amaranthine,
Holding it, to make it forever mine

Beyond our perceptual faraway and thoughts,
Infusing with sedulity that simply ought

Convalescing that belief with their morality,
Saving the blind, who often subject to pity.

REPUTATION

Vacillating I reach at a point in my life,
Losing my molimentum is what it's like?

Steady not slowly, it will subsume,
Unceasing that process recoiling as loop

Don't lose heart, keep moving Simran,
It's a parcel of life, stay put in the run
Sturdy as they say it's easy said than done

I dread and feel what if I'm losing that thread?
Benevolence says it's all up in my head

Mere thoughts won't aid in any which way,
everyone has their own feet of clay
Keep a stiff upper lip before get into a play

Point well taken, I forgather what lost,
Swear I shall win, no matter what cost

Guard my thoughts and lead towards light,
Boat that adrifted, will regain its might.

PUGNACIOUS LOVE

I knew this path is gonna be tough
But thought to sooth it, no matter how rough

Luring from peripheral, the fulcrum of this journey is scary
Tried to make out one, felt far from merry

Dint anticipate a bump too soon in a process
Once again makes me villain, wonder how they prowess

Perhaps, I am the one who put cart before the horse
Thinking that might save my sane, is a thought to recourse

Servilely thinking! Is this what I deserve?
Sabotaging my belief and standing on my nerve?

Oh mighty! Save me from diminishing of my worth
Exhausted ad nauseam, stop burgeon forth

But love is truly peculiar in its ways
all about let loosing one yet we hold it like a bale of hay

In quest to get, we overleap to get down to brass tacks
Expunging the sensitivity not-knowing that we don't know diddly-squat

Failed to understand what comprises this coalition
Terribly inter - linking - lacing - locking and woven!
Where is the f**king equation?

Oh no no please ! I have tasted this shit many a times,
More of this game is of echoing, then of rhymes

Oh yes! I understand love is like pubg
Not at all dangerous until you play,
As reaching terminus ad quem, you will be snatched from your lee

Yes ! my thoughts are raptured and not wise,
Wait, until I experience otherwise

HOLDING TIGHT

Harum scarum when I entered here,
So heedless with mind so bare

Desirous of what not, my demeanour was in pell-mell,
Slowly and steadily, I tried to break that shell

Colligating the fact that sky's the limit,
It's the way you take, requiring no licence no permit

What can I say now! Too far I have reached, yet not satiated,
Am I drifted or off the beaten track?

Via stumbling or fumbling, whatever little I have attained,
God knows how true I am, and how far to sustain?

Back-down wanted to try, but my hands were fastened,
Agonising the value of time, I could have hastened,
But now can't cry over spilled milk, this foul-up is
beyond chastened

I feel like losing every breath of my breathe,
vision is glaze-over with no vibrating reed
Holding tight till it too become creep

May forgather what lost, hoping this damage
can be mitigated,
coz, too far i have come, yet not satiated
Am I drifted or off the beaten track?
Perhaps ! Just SALUS IN ARDUIS is what I lack !!!

MY FOOTWEARS

Oh! my ballerinas and oh! my boots,
Residing in the shelf, so is my boost

I know you crave to walk around,
Up and down, experience the beauty in bound
Alas! things not ok, please wait and ground

Don't worry, I am with you,
I heard patience pays well, lets not hound

You know my relentless love for you,
I have one in green, black, silver and blue

My stilettos! You are the queen of my footwear,
Intimated with you ad-infinitum, I shall swear

Agreed! It's been a while I touched you,,
Situation so haec, I'm myself in rue

My knee length gumboots, you better buck up
Monsoon at the corner, lets together sum up

It's strange how we befriended each other, my mules,
Cavalier of your gemutlich of which I had no clues

I hope this time shall pass al tiro,
You rest with your lustre intact, pro tempore

THANK YOU!

Thank you for giving me these experiences,
Oblivious I was, inadvertently in eff and blind
Wasting my time thinking those words in rewind

Wondering if this what I ever ought to get,
Refuse to receive, I rather shoot them at sight

Penetrating under my skin and sucking my peace,
Should I be worried or jump in glee?
Thank you! Accept my pardon is all I plea

Confidence is butchered and attempts are doubted,
Reality check! My lessons of dura-vita has debuted

I welcome my self to this world of intense
narcissism,
Belittling again and time in its many schisms

A thought of being thoughtful has gone ages back,
But confessionally, I am dreadful ad infinitum of giving
the sack

Who I am and how far I can stretch?
Believing in my belief system and valuing my values is all I fetch

This life is a muddle for poor and rich,
Winner is one who triumph this kettle of fish

But the one in the game is effete to assess,
Thank you for giving me these experiences, I now know to handle this mess

Vulnerably, I feel like silently crying in my clamorous mind,
Maybe I'm at fault, let's settle this kind

Yes they say that path to success is not easy,
Withal in name of this success , god knows how many
lives have blown out of the water
Gosh! It's a vicious circle, one better fit to cater

As I fail to understand the point of terminus,
Is it a bed of roses with a cherry on a cake?
Or an infinite treasure that we ultimately are gonna take?

If I now know my metier, it's not a bad deal in exchange.
Its poor to die on the vine than on stage

Thank you for giving me these experiences,
Coz, I adhere life is all what you make

BACK OFF

There is no right or wrong, its all grey,
The choices are either be slayer or be prey
Stage is set! C'mon lets play

But is this all about winning or losing?
What about populist like me who are poor players?
Take the dare else ready for smear

Trust me! I am zonked playing this game,
Can't let go my scruples in flames

This sheer rivalrous won't take us far,
Scathing the fabric of life, leaving a perennial scar

Hitherto, I haven't found the middle route
Where there is no victorem or dud,
Where serenity in mind and benignity in actions take root

So what damn it ! So what if I don't reach that focal,
Being canonical than pseudo could be the proposal
With foots in motley, I'm choreographing my
own Paso doble

Have I asked too much and too early?
Or may be my asking is unjust as I was asking merely

I know! Life is to explore and to each one its own,
Omnis garnish there life melodies with different tones,
However, in this disorderly haste I know, I am not alone.

MY MULISH WEIGHT

Oh my weight, this shouldn't be done,
Why do you do this to me and refuse to shun?

Calibrating every single morsel I eat
Abstaining from sweets, stayed away from meat,
Ok fine! I confess at times I cheat

My staple is incapable to invite you,
Much displeased! Is it my water that keeps you in woo?

My walk and sprint is out of breath,
Your mulishness is subject to fret

What not I have done to keep you in check?
Ages gone for my last chic look, blooming heck !!!

Flagrantly you creep in, where not to be described,
Tell me what you need - barter or bribe?

Hope you understand what you mean to this world,
An inch corpulent and there you be twirl

Just like all, your genuineness would be impugned,
Still not spared, your appearance would be judged

Excess of anything is bad but you, is extremely one
You sucked all run even from Simran,
Look ! I'm serious and no more fun
Nothing left now, i'm out of this scrum

My gibbose bespeak of your unsought exhibit,
Oh my Weight ! your disappearance is least I solicit !

TRAPPED

Pavidus like child who express mirth when
not in school,
When teacher is absent, she is out of rule

Reluctant in undertaking any endeavours,
Fearing that may justify the perceptions of so called
superiors

Obtaining utmost felicity in my own nest,
Where I can jump and ramble, not thinking about
the rest

My shack is my new happy zone,
unlike others, its far being judgmental prone

But Trust me! I am imbrued in this shuddery,
Shackled in this turf, yearning to set free

Treed in a situation where doing does more harm then not doing,
Assailable my spirit, can't end up ruing

At times I stagger in fright,
yet self-complacent, wrong and nor right

Unfeignedly! I am sitting in the corner waiting for my turn,
Before my soul ceases crash and burn

All I turn this anger into a humble pray,
Oh god ! Release me from this abominable stray

FART

Few things are brooked, solely when done by you,
irregardless how much it make others' askew

Such is a relation of mine with my fart,
Sloppy I am, let me clear this in start

For me, you are my silent garrulous gassy friend,
Except for the times when you get sonic and make others upend

What you make of others thrust me! I don't give a hoot,
Turning trickle into gusher is all in their root
But who are we to feed, coz that one fart is for them to breathe!

Your olfactory sensation informs me of my interiors,
At times I frui momento, at times derelict but ne'er inferior

I remember when you came audible in front of my boss,
More than i, it turned him rueful to come across
Flukily! Considering it an innocuous prank, he gave it a toss

The night in an aircraft, when crowd went on crusade,
Blaming that poor for what environ he made,
Diffused in malodorous gases, even I lament why I came

Withal recalling many evenings roaming in that lane,
Releasing me, from that unendurable pain
Can't defy your power to keep us sane
Oh! now I know you know how to be freed,
Perhaps one fart is all we need

You are mine is the only fact that I care the most
if, of someone else's, I would have given up the ghost

It's ok my fart, anywhere anytime, I'm ready to claver,
That's the unicity of our bond, which is forever

RESTLESS SOUL

Today I discover something in me-
What I have and what I will be

I'm 30, single and mind-numbing,
Aboveboard ! vestal and flagrantly sucking

My routine is humdrum and I'm stuck somewhere,
Expiring per diem, as if I don't care
Or maybe it's a beginning, I am wet behind the ears

Tempus in hand, I know, is cardinal,
But my vigor is low and mind marginal

At times I'm freewheeling, at times pensive,
Whatever it is, I have no apprehensive

Commencing with a lie, I do not know my tomorrow,
But my parents are proud and that I dint borrow

However, there is a certainty in my uncertain tomorrow,
Waking up with aspirations, I am, each morrow,
With my drudgery, which is modest and narrow

Messing with my half baked ideas which are still half,
though!
Don't know if I turn up trumps or being faugh

I wonder if is it all worth or I'm in semblance,
Well! these are mere talks, I'm still on the fence

Or perhaps! we have to lend time some time,
As somewhere I don't care now even if I turn a nice dime

Leaving everything I wanted to go too far,
Unreached I become, fostering my new avatar

Where I square - off my position of me
What I have and what I will be

COME BACK

Vagrant I was, until I found you,
Prolix, until I listened you,
And benighted, until I experienced you

Distance doesn't matter, if intent is hitting straight,
Remembering those converses when I was insanely irate

Our folksy talks are like rechargeable pills,
Unrestrained that process, until in each other we spill

Amassing the gumption of knowing the world,
I wasn't alone, we sailed it together
Suffering from same mental impairment, that we
thoroughly savour

No matter how peculiar or chagrined, we unleash every
single thought
Our habitué is all that saved us from the nought

Watered my imagination and gimbaled my modest ideas,
Who are you - a friend or embody of abundantia?

Reverence for you is not for your age, but humility,
Have run-across many hitherto, none matches your civility
If viable, i may pilfer this in best of my ability

Yes ! Time so hard-hitting, we better restore our vim,
Tempus et transient, even the darkest of the dim

Hey! Take all in your stride and toss it away,
You know it's all in our heads, strike back hard
from your way

You have been a fighter, I know you will this time too,
Remember ! You have got your work cut out for you

Praying for the speedy convalescence with no other tense,
Someone Waiting from the other side of the fence!

(Dedicated to my late friend whom
I lost dated Sep 16, 2020)

FOREVER IN ME

I wish to whisper you what it's like
Standing beside, numb and psyche,
And figuring out what's next,
from life which has taken us, in wrest

No it's tough, weeping my heart and soul so
drift apart,
Coz now my life is worth a drat

Hey! Get up, listen and talk to me,
With you I somehow can be

There were still many miles to go and springs to takes,
Marooned me amidst this, for Pete's sake

You knew that no man is an island
Bequeath me with spate of sorrowful glands,
Fine! Then wait until I drop by the wayside and disband

You knew my reasons of bare-knuckle and
atremble,
Yet set forth far and left me to walk this rundle

But remember! This asunder won't take you out of me,
Rather, commemorate henceforth in my acerbic and glee,
As without you I'm semper incomplete...